The Picture Story of
THE PHILIPPINES

BY HESTER O'NEILL

PICTURES BY URSULA KOERING

THE JUNIOR LITERARY GUILD · NEW YORK
AND
DAVID McKAY COMPANY · PHILADELPHIA

Fourth of July across the Pacific

For many years the Fourth of July has been an exciting day to the boys and girls who live in the cities of the Philippines—that long chain of bright green tropical islands, stretched along the coast of south China. Firecrackers from China were shot off from early morning until sundown. There were parades with trumpeting bands. At night the starry tropical skies were filled with bursting rockets, bright flares, and the falling stars of night fireworks. Filipino boys and girls always stayed up late to watch them and help celebrate American Independence Day.

The first time Fourth of July was celebrated in the Philippines was around 1900, when the American Army and Navy took over the Philippines from Spain. At that time Spain had held the islands for about four hundred years. From the time the United States began to govern the Philippines, the President of the United States promised the Filipino people that, when they were ready to govern themselves, they would be set free. The United States kept its promise. And that is why, in 1946,

the greatest Fourth of July ever celebrated in the Philippines took place. On that day, Fourth of July became Philippine Independence Day too, and for the first time in hundreds of years Filipinos were free men and women and boys and girls, exactly like Americans.

On the great Fourth of July of 1946 there were no firecrackers. The beautiful capital city of Manila lay in ruins. There were only a few of its big buildings still standing after the terrible war with Japan which had just been fought in the streets of Manila. But on wide Dewey Boulevard, named for the American admiral who had won these islands from Spain, an enormous grandstand looking out over Manila's wide bay had been built. Filipino boys and girls came from all Manila, and in from the rice paddies and down from the mountains with their fathers and mothers to watch the new president, Manuel Roxas, whom they had just elected, raise the Philippine flag to the top of its standard, while all over the islands bells rang to celebrate the first Philippine Independence Day.

16012

Living in a nipa house

In the smaller cities and little country towns, called "barrios," Filipinos sometimes live in "nipa" homes. These are built in a very special way for hot countries. Their name comes from the nipa rush-thatched roof, and they are the coolest kind of house to live in. The earliest type of nipa houses ever built in the Philippines is still used in the small villages and country fields. There are some around the edges of the capital city of Manila, too. Often the nipa houses belong to fishermen's families, and are built right out over the water with a "banca" or "casco" or outrigger canoe, tied underneath on the water. Even on dry ground, houses are built up on bamboo stilts. The sides are of bamboo, and so are the floors. Windowpanes are usually made of seashells instead of glass. The sliding windows can be opened down to the floor to catch all the breeze. In one of the windows of the nipa house, swinging in a coconut shell vase, a fresh orchid plant always hangs. These lovely flowers grow wild in nearby jungles. In America this precious orchid plant would be very expensive. But Filipino flower sellers often give them away to anyone buying a peseta's worth of marigolds or some other flower just as common in America.

Everything is planned to keep these nipa houses as cool as possible in the warm climate. Furniture is very simple. It is made of the same kind of bamboo and rattan as the house. The beds are usually just smooth flat straw mats on the floor, and they can be rolled up and put in a corner during the day. It is easy to keep a nipa house clean, for the smooth shiny bamboo floors are laid with little spaces between each split bamboo pole. Whenever the Filipina housewife sweeps her floor, all the dirt on it falls through these little slits onto the ground below. Crumbs are picked up by the chickens and pigs, which in the poorer homes live underneath the house. In other homes, chickens and pigs sleep in their own bamboo pens near the house.

The small porch, like a balcony, is covered also by the nipa-thatched roof. It is a pleasant place to sing in the evening, while one of the family plays on his guitar or ukulele. There may be several musical instruments in even the smallest nipa house, for all Filipinos love music.

In the dry part of the year, nipa houses catch fire very easily and burn down quickly. But the family can find all the new material it needs just a few steps away. And it is not long before a new nipa house has been built, with the help of the neighbors, right where the old one was. Much of the food the family eats is just a few steps away from the house, too, perhaps on its own land. This food comes from banana, coconut, mango and papaya trees. Rice, the main food of the country, is grown in nearby paddies. The waters are full of fish which are good to eat. When they are not in school, Filipino boys and girls help with the gardens, and take care of the chickens and pigs. They drive the carabaos to the fields, brandishing a stick at them if they try to go the wrong way.

Land of the carabao

The most familiar sight everywhere in the Philippines is the big awkward lumbering work animal, the heavy-horned "carabao" or water buffalo. These are fierce animals until they are tamed, but then even the very small Filipino boys handle them easily. It is not unusual to see a small Filipino caretaker curled up sound asleep against the haunch of a carabao, while the big beast lies on the ground. Carabaos draw the plows in the country fields, and they haul heavily loaded wooden wagons even through the city streets of Manila. They are used for meat, they give milk to drink, and their horns are made into the "tambuli," which hangs beside the door of each nipa house. When this hollow horn is blown, it can be heard for a great distance. If fishing boats are in trouble at sea or someone is lost in the mountains, the tambuli is blown and help can be sent. This horn is so important that only the father of the house ever blows it, and small Filipino boys wait eagerly for the day when they will be grown up enough to blow the tambuli.

Carabaos think they must have a mudbath every day. When they come to mud-holes, they lie right down in them, no matter what else they are supposed to be doing, and wallow around until they are cooled off. Then they are willing to go back to work again.

A BANCA

A BANCA WITH OUTRIGGER AND SAIL

And land of boats

If you look down from a plane on the bright blue waters of the tropical South Pacific Ocean, you will see another typical Filipino sight. All the waters between and around the islands seem filled with square sails every color of the rainbow. These sails are fastened on tall bamboo poles to outrigger canoes, scudding across the waters of the islands, their bright sails snapped out in soft tropic breezes. Outriggers are long bamboo poles fastened to the edge of the canoe. They stick out over the water to steady the boat in huge ocean swells. Sometimes the sails of outrigger canoes will be made of many colors, and other times they will have sails of just one bright color.

Many Filipinos make their living by fishing, and they go out to sea in fast boats they call "vintas," which usually have matting sails. Another kind of Filipino boat is called a "casco." This is a little dugout canoe with an arched matting roof over the middle. There are big "lorchas" too, pushed along by thirty-foot bamboo poles. And there are little bancas. For oars—if they do not have regular one-piece wooden oars—Filipinos use a square board tied to the end of a bamboo pole by rattan. They can easily make these oars themselves. Filipino boys learn to swim and to handle all these boats when they are very young.

A VINTA

A CASCO

School and play

Filipino boys and girls like the same games that you do. The girls play hop-scotch and call it "kit-kit." The boys play marbles, and there is a game with marbles in holes in a board like Chinese checkers. This is called "chonka." They all like to play musical chairs, and hide and seek, too. The yoyo, bouncing up and down on its string, is one of their special games, exactly like yours. Older boys and girls like to play basketball and indoor baseball. The boys play soccer football and "sipa," which is a game played with a hollow rattan ball as big as a soft-ball, kicked back and forth by the players, who make a circle.

It was the Americans who brought the schools as they are today to the Philippines. In 1900, when the American Army and the Filipinos stopped fighting each other and the Philippines became a possession of the United States, American soldiers put down their guns and took up schoolbooks instead. They gathered together groups of small Filipino boys and girls to teach them about the United States. As a boy, Manuel Roxas, the first president of the Philippine Republic, learned English sitting on an American soldier's knee. The soldiers taught the boys and girls until a whole boatload of teachers could be sent out from the United States.

If you went into a Filipino schoolroom now, you would find that the boys and girls have Filipino teachers, many of them taught by those first Americans. Boys and girls study the same lessons that you do, from many of the same books printed in the United States. Because of the large exports of embroidered articles from the Philippines, girls usually have special classes in embroidery. But Filipino boys and girls go to school at a different time of year than you do. Their long vacation is in April and May, during the hottest months. Their school year begins in June, and it is not divided into semesters. There is a long vacation at Christmas, and they have the same holidays that you do. In Manila, some boys and girls eat lunches prepared at school. Out in the country, if they live too far away to go home for lunch, they take it with them in little hand-woven baskets. Usually, it is rice and dried fish and fruit. Others, who live nearer to their school, are able to go home for their noonday meal.

Before the Americans came, the Spaniards had church schools, and there are still many church schools on the islands. There are quite a few colleges, too. The best known of these is Santo Tomas in Manila, which the Spaniards opened in 1611. It is twenty-five years older than Harvard, which is the oldest college in the United States. The Americans who were living in the Philippines when the Japanese invaded it in 1941, came to know the inside of Santo Tomas very well: they were kept prisoners of the Japanese in Santo Tomas until the war was over.

While they are in the lower grades, Filipino boys and girls begin to think about what they want to be when they grow up, just as you do. Many boys study to become lawyers, because they are interested in serving their country in its government, and they know that studying law helps them to do this. Some boys and girls go to college in Europe and America when they finish school in the Philippines. Girls study the same things American girls do, to prepare themselves for the same kinds of work. Some of the boys and girls go to business schools. Others go to the big agricultural colleges to learn how to be good farmers.

Many years ago, while Spain still governed the islands, a Filipino boy became one of the most famous doctors in the world. Men from all countries came to him for treatment, and famous doctors all over the world made him their friend. He decided, as a boy, to be a doctor when his mother became blind, because there were so few doctors in the Philippines at that time. He studied hard in the Philippines and Europe, traveling, too, in the United States. Then he came back to his own country and did a wonderful eye operation on his mother so that she was able to see once more. This man was José Rizal, the great Filipino patriot who spent his entire short life working for the welfare of his country. He wrote great books about the hardships of the Filipino people in those days. Now his name is in every city and barrio in the islands. Parks and buildings are named after him. So are many streets and schools.

In the public schools, you will find the same pictures of Washington and Lincoln which hang on your school walls. There is always a picture, too, of José Rizal. Each morning, school begins with the flag ceremony and the singing of the Filipino national anthem, "Land of the morning, Child of the sun returning. . . ."

The capital city of this bright land of the morning, Manila, spreads for fourteen square miles along the flat shores of Manila Bay on the big island of Luzon in the north of the island chain. It faces toward China. In the days before the war with Japan, it was one of the biggest ports for ships in the world, and a gay busy city that was really made up of three different cities.

One of these was the old Spanish walled town. It was named "Intramuros," which means between walls. The high old gray stone walls, built so many hundreds of years ago by the Spaniards, made a circle of two and a half miles. Long ago, this was surrounded by a wide moat. After the Americans came, they filled in this moat with earth, and planted trees and flowers over it to make a wide park all around Intramuros. Here bloomed bright flame trees, brilliant bougainvillea, cannas, hibiscus bushes of all different colors, and white gardenia-like "sampaguitas"—the national flower of the Philippines.

The second city was the American city, with busy department stores and offices side by side with the little open-front shops of Chinese merchants. This part of Manila had big modern apartment houses, beautiful theatres, the large high-ceilinged, air-cooled Manila Hotel, and the Army and Navy Club down by the waterfront near another beautiful park called the Luneta. This had once been a big field, about twice the size of a football field, by the sea, where Filipino patriots, José Rizal included, had been shot by the Spaniards. The Americans made it into a park instead, and in the warm tropic nights it was always crowded with Manila people driving, all in the same direction, around and around its big circle of a drive, or sitting on the grass listening to band concerts.

The third city was made up of the bamboo and nipa-roofed houses along the shore where the fisher folk lived. These were built only around the fringes of Manila because they catch fire so easily. Many of them were built up on high bamboo stilts right over the waters of wide Manila Bay.

A beautiful capital

The Japanese destroyed most of Manila before they were driven out by the Americans and Filipinos in the early winter of 1945. The old Spanish city is almost completely gone and can never be rebuilt. But the Filipinos went to work at once to build up their modern capital city, even though they knew it would take them a long long time, for Manila was the most destroyed of all the big cities of the world during the war.

The city that the Japanese bombed and burned so completely was one of the gayest cities in the world before the war. If you came into it by plane, green islands with brown spots, which were mountain peaks, first loomed out of the bright blue sea. The flooded rice paddies on the hillsides looked like thin lines of pale green lying in terraces of mirrors. This was caused by the sunshine on the flooded fields of rice. All the shades of green that you have ever seen were in the colors of the tree tops as the plane winged over the islands, dark green tufts of mango trees, lacy green patches of bamboo, and the great waving fingers of all kinds of palm trees, and the black-green patches of jungles.

As your plane dipped low over Manila Bay two outstretched arms of land reached out to meet you, one of them the big American Naval base at Cavite, and the other covered with the mountain ridges of Bataan. In the middle of the bay jutted up toward the skies the enormous rock of Corregidor, the inside of which was a giant honeycomb of storerooms and fortifications. It was here that Filipinos and Americans made their last valiant stand against the Japanese invaders.

It was beautiful to come into Manila Bay by ship, too. The white buildings sparkled across the bay, with bright sunshine glinting on their columns, red tile roofs and huge windows, covered with iron grillwork. The docks toward which your ship pointed were lined with huge boats from all over the world and covered with men and machines loading and unloading cargoes day and night.

Once on land in Manila after the long trip, exploring the city itself was great fun, for you never knew what new sight would meet your eyes. Traffic was often snarled by a big cream-colored bull drawing a rumbling rickety cart across a narrow canal bridge, while the driver of a big shining American car behind him shouted at him to hurry out of the way. If you were in that car and happened to be stalled behind the slow carts right on the top of a hump-backed bridge, you would while away the time you had to wait for the road to clear, by watching all the traffic on the canal underneath. Here traffic jams were caused by water hyacinths tangling in the poles of the boatmen as they ferried loads of mangoes or tiny finger bananas or coconuts to market on their canal barges.

As in American cities, the houses of Manila were all sizes, some with large formal gardens and others with small dusky half-wild gardens. The houses themselves were made up of many different kinds of architecture, a combination of American, Spanish and Filipino. Their floors were either of the cool figured Spanish tiles, which were easy to keep clean, or made of the beautiful mahogany

wood of the islands. Most of them had Spanish iron grillwork at the windows and in balconies, and low overhanging roofs kept out the scorching midday sun.

In the evenings when the sun had gone down, the city was alive with pleasant ways to pass the time. Radio stations broadcast the kind of music that Filipino people enjoy most—romantic songs and symphonies. A pleasant custom of the islands was to call on friends in the evening, and talk and sing on the steps of the houses visited. There was a big air-cooled movie theatre called the Ideal, where American movies could be seen, and many smaller theatres which ran both American and Filipino movies. There was a huge theatre where elaborate Filipino plays were given. These were usually allegories or romances, with many jokes and puns which had to do with the life in the islands. After the movies and plays, people could go to soda fountains just as you do, or ice cream stores, or they could go to a restaurant for a late meal of any kind they wished. There were, as in all large cities, many

different kinds of restaurants serving the food of many different countries—a Chinese dinner to be had under the stars on the roof of the Oriental Hotel, French food in a beautiful airy balconied spot. The restaurants had either American or Filipino orchestras. When traveling opera companies came to Manila, they played to packed houses, for the Filipino people love opera. In the audiences there was always a sprinkling of American and English people who lived in Manila. And many times East Indians could be seen in handsome robes, the East Indian women often wearing diamonds in their noses.

Coming home in the evening from all of these pleasant things to do, the balmy tropical air was heavy with the scent of flowers everywhere, often with the fragrant and delicate "Dama de la Noche," Lady of the Night.

This, then, was the happy city of Manila which its people are now working to rebuild, as well as their churches, hospitals, schools and libraries.

The busy Pasig River

Through Manila flows one of the busiest rivers in the world. And that is how the city of Manila got its name. The Pasig River is covered with a pale green cabbage-like plant called "nila." At first Manila was called Maynila, and the "may" meant "there are." So Maynila meant "There are the nilas." A big lake, covered in the rainy season with pale pink lotus blossoms, lies in Rizal Province near Manila. Hundreds of little boats make their way from this lake, Laguna de Bay, back and forth along the river from dawn until dark, bringing tropical fruits, chickens and vegetables and other food down to the city markets of Manila. Big rafts, made by tying coconuts together, often float down the river. The coconut rafts will be piled high with coconuts, too, and on top of the pile the owner of the raft can be seen peacefully asleep in the sun on his long ride down the river. José Rizal once said that the Pasig was busier than the Hudson River in America. He thought the Pasig was the busiest river in the world—and he had lived in many different parts of the world. The Pasig can almost be called one of Manila's main streets.

THE RIGODON

The Malacañan Palace

In the middle of beautiful gardens along the shore of the Pasig River is the Malacañan Palace. It was built hundreds of years ago as the home for the Spanish governors of the Philippines. In the days of the Spanish rule, its great iron gates were locked and no Filipino was ever allowed to enter. After the Americans came, the Commander of the United States Army lived at Malacañan. Then when Judge Taft was made governor of the Philippines, he lived there. For the first time in all the hundreds of years that Malacañan had been the seat of the Philippine government, the gates were thrown open and Filipinos were welcome. Judge Taft invited Filipinos to his parties. He was the first governor of the Philippines to do so, except for one Spanish governor who had been there a very short time many many years before. Since 1935, a Filipino has lived in Malacañan. The first one was Manuel Quezon, who was elected by Filipino men and women to be the first president of the Commonwealth while it was still governed by the United States. It was a day of great rejoicing in all the islands of the Philippines when Manuel Quezon entered the door of the beautiful official house of his country, and after centuries, it was at last to be lived in by Filipinos.

MALACAÑAN PALACE

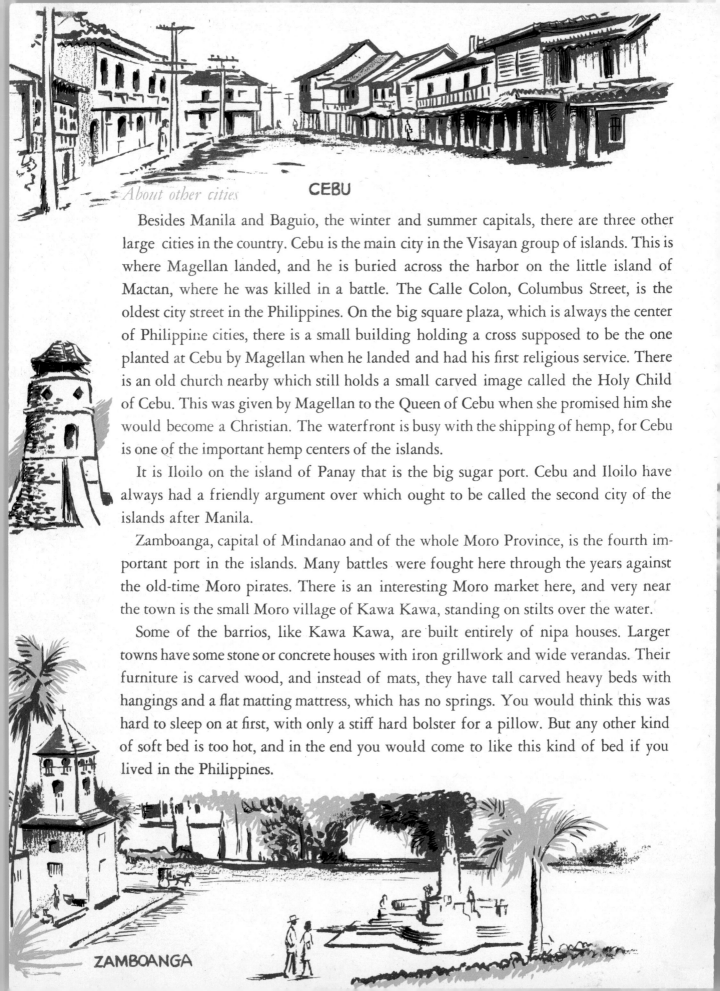

CEBU

Besides Manila and Baguio, the winter and summer capitals, there are three other large cities in the country. Cebu is the main city in the Visayan group of islands. This is where Magellan landed, and he is buried across the harbor on the little island of Mactan, where he was killed in a battle. The Calle Colon, Columbus Street, is the oldest city street in the Philippines. On the big square plaza, which is always the center of Philippine cities, there is a small building holding a cross supposed to be the one planted at Cebu by Magellan when he landed and had his first religious service. There is an old church nearby which still holds a small carved image called the Holy Child of Cebu. This was given by Magellan to the Queen of Cebu when she promised him she would become a Christian. The waterfront is busy with the shipping of hemp, for Cebu is one of the important hemp centers of the islands.

It is Iloilo on the island of Panay that is the big sugar port. Cebu and Iloilo have always had a friendly argument over which ought to be called the second city of the islands after Manila.

Zamboanga, capital of Mindanao and of the whole Moro Province, is the fourth important port in the islands. Many battles were fought here through the years against the old-time Moro pirates. There is an interesting Moro market here, and very near the town is the small Moro village of Kawa Kawa, standing on stilts over the water.

Some of the barrios, like Kawa Kawa, are built entirely of nipa houses. Larger towns have some stone or concrete houses with iron grillwork and wide verandas. Their furniture is carved wood, and instead of mats, they have tall carved heavy beds with hangings and a flat matting mattress, which has no springs. You would think this was hard to sleep on at first, with only a stiff hard bolster for a pillow. But any other kind of soft bed is too hot, and in the end you would come to like this kind of bed if you lived in the Philippines.

ZAMBOANGA

A year of only two seasons — the rainy and the dry

The hottest months of the year in the tropical Philippines are April and May. December, January and February are the nicest months. From June to December comes the rainy season. It does not rain all of the time in the rainy season, of course. But it rains quite hard nearly every day for part of the day. There is a very special kind of storm in that part of the world. These are the big wind and rain storms known on the Atlantic side of the world as hurricanes. In the Pacific, hurricanes are called typhoons. Windowpanes of seashells are so strong that the big winds cannot blow them in. Over the windows are straw awnings, called "sawalis." When a sudden typhoon comes up, Filipinos rush to their windows, pull out the sticks which have braced the awnings away from the houses. In a second the sawalis have dropped flat against the wall and the sliding windows are held tight against the blows of the storm.

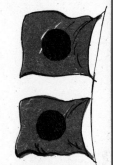

HURRICANE WARNING

16012

Washing on the river banks

Because of the warm climate, Filipino people like to bathe, and they do this so often that they are among the cleanest people in the world. All over the islands are hot springs in which people bathe. And wherever you travel around the country, you will see women kneeling along the banks of the small mountain rivers, washing clothes against the stones. There will be people bathing in the rivers too, and sometimes you will see someone drive a carabao into the river and wash off its thick hide. This is supposed to calm its nerves.

The women who wash clothes in the city are called "lavanderas." Many of them have electric irons just like the one in your house. Others use big irons filled with burning charcoal. Out in the country they sometimes use just plain flat irons which they heat on hot stones. In Manila, the lavanderas come for the laundry in horse-drawn carriages and bring it back that way, too.

Gardens in steps — the rice terraces

Just as carabaos and nipa houses and fiestas always make people think at once of the Philippines whenever they hear them mentioned, so does rice, for that is the main food of the Filipino people.

Mountains and lowlands of all of the islands are covered with rice paddies. Because the country is warm all of the time, there can be three crops of rice harvested each year.

There is a wonderful sight up in the mountains outside of Manila in the Ifugao country. It is like nothing else in the world. Many hundreds of years ago, early Filipinos built tremendous high terraces up the sides of the mountains there, although they had nothing but their bolo knives with which to hack out the stone sides of the mountains. On each separate terrace is a flooded field of rice, used today just as it was when the terraces were first built. High ladders, standing hundreds of feet straight up into the air reach from one terrace to another. This is the only way people can get from one rice field to the next one.

Rice planting in the islands is always a busy time. The whole family helps in each rice paddy. The land is plowed with a small wooden hand plow, which has a sharp steel point. This is drawn slowly around by a carabao. The first little pale green shoots grown from the seeds are put by hand, one stalk at a time, into a muddy flooded field. Everyone in the family helps again at the harvest time. Then the rice stalks are tied up like haystacks. Each one has a piece of red cloth on it to bring luck in a big harvest. After the stalks are dry enough, threshing time begins.

There are always gay dances at the harvest time, and singing to the dancing. Many dances are about the rice itself—the Rice Planting dance and song which begins, "Planting rice is never fun," and the Salakot dance, named for the wide bamboo and rattan hat which everyone wears in the rice fields to protect himself from the sun. In the evening, when the hard day's work is done, the men sit in a circle and strum on their musical instruments, while the girls dance the rice festival dances.

To market, to market

Most of the rice is sent to large cities like Manila to be shipped out of the country or sold in the market. Here rice is measured out by the "ganta," which is about two pounds. There are fruit and vegetable vendors, too, who come through the streets of Manila, crying their wares and selling from their little carts. Everyone goes to market to buy most of the day's food early in the morning before it is time for the siesta in the hottest part of the day. There are several of these big markets in Manila because it is such a large city. These markets are wide spaces of ground under corrugated tin roofs which keep off the hot tropic sun. The markets in the country towns are the same, except their roofs are the nipa-thatched roofs. All of the tropical fruits, meats, fish and vegetables sold in Manila are brought in from the country packed in Spanish moss. Often bolts of hand-woven cloth are sold in the food markets, too. Live chickens cackle busily over the voices of the people.

You would like to shop around the noisy markets with your bright woven basket on your arm for the many fruits that are

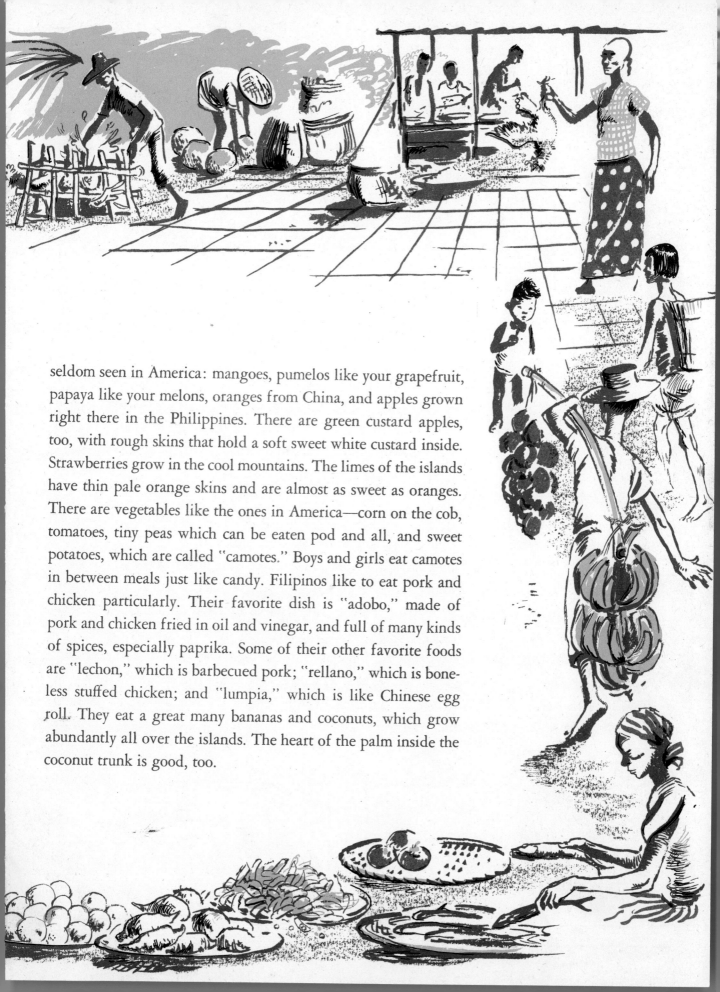

seldom seen in America: mangoes, pumelos like your grapefruit, papaya like your melons, oranges from China, and apples grown right there in the Philippines. There are green custard apples, too, with rough skins that hold a soft sweet white custard inside. Strawberries grow in the cool mountains. The limes of the islands have thin pale orange skins and are almost as sweet as oranges. There are vegetables like the ones in America—corn on the cob, tomatoes, tiny peas which can be eaten pod and all, and sweet potatoes, which are called "camotes." Boys and girls eat camotes in between meals just like candy. Filipinos like to eat pork and chicken particularly. Their favorite dish is "adobo," made of pork and chicken fried in oil and vinegar, and full of many kinds of spices, especially paprika. Some of their other favorite foods are "lechon," which is barbecued pork; "rellano," which is boneless stuffed chicken; and "lumpia," which is like Chinese egg roll. They eat a great many bananas and coconuts, which grow abundantly all over the islands. The heart of the palm inside the coconut trunk is good, too.

A fifty-cent American dollar

The money that changes hands in the daily shopping in the markets is much like American money. Just as we have American silver dollars, but use paper ones most of the time, so do the Filipinos have paper "pesos." They look very much like the United States bills, with a big PHILIPPINES printed across them.

The metal money, like American half-dollars, quarters, dimes, nickels, and pennies, are "centavos." The one-centavo is copper, but much bigger than the American penny. The other centavos are silver. They are about the same size as American money of the same amount. The twenty-centavo piece is called a "peseta," and is a little smaller than the quarter. The fifty-centavo piece is the size of the United States fifty-cent piece, and the silver peso dollar has the same figure and seal of the Philippines as the smaller silver pieces.

The big silver pesos, which the Spanish galleons used to bring back from Mexico in the long-ago days, were used in the Philippines even after the Americans took over its government. They still kept the name, peso, and although it was a Filipino dollar, it took two pesos to make an American dollar. That is why people used to ask each other riddles about "the fifty-cent American dollar." The answer to these riddles was the Philippine peso.

When the Japanese invaded the Philippines, they tried to capture all Philippine money and make the people use Japanese money. Filipinos used to call this worthless money "Mickey Mouse money." But the Japanese never were able to capture the gold, for the Philippine government and the American Army secretly saved it. They took it away on an American submarine, and it was kept safely in Washington, D. C., all through the war until the Japanese were at last driven away from the Philippines. To keep the paper pesos away from the Japanese invaders, the government burned all the paper money in the big tunneled fortress of Corregidor at the entrance to Manila Bay. With bombs falling all around, the men bravely tended the big bonfire of burning money to keep it from their enemy.

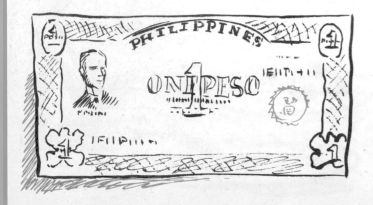

The Filipino with a small farm usually has only one paying crop. He ploughs, plants, harvests and threshes his rice and takes it to market. The money he gets for it may be all that the family has to last through the year. Fortunately, a lot of things to eat are free. A mango tree in the yard, a bamboo thicket nearby, coconuts from down the road, all these help feed the family. And even herbs for stew grow in the fields. The farmer's carabao and goat and pigs eat rice-hay and family leftovers.

Fishermen use boats that have long bamboo poles to hold up the nets.

Everywhere in the Philippines you will see the long strands of hemp for rope hung out to dry on fences in the shade of coconut trees. It looks like hanks of bright hair. From the leaves of the abaca plant come the long hemp threads which are dried and then twisted into Manila rope. The threads are loosened from the leaves by a little machine, worked with a foot pedal, which draws a knife across the leaves.

This is a big gold mine in the mountains of Luzon. Some iron is mined, too.

Here you can see a boat being built.

Whirring sawmills cut up many kinds of trees into wood for beautiful colored floors and furniture.

The coconut palm

The most famous tree in the Philippines is the coconut. With the coconut tree and a bamboo grove and the nipa plant, Filipinos can live without almost anything else, for they use nearly every inch of these plants for something. It is nothing for a Filipino boy to shinny quickly up the tall trunk of a coconut tree and cut down some fresh coconuts to eat and to drink the water inside. Out of the leaves, which they call "dahon," Filipinos weave men's hats and often women's too, slippers, braid, fans, and handbags. From the big midrib of the leaf they make brooms. They call the coco shell "bao ng niyog." From this they make cups, lampshades, buckles, buttons, ash trays and a kind of product which helps preserve wood. They make charcoal and briquets out of this too. From the coconut husk, Filipinos make yarn, kitchen brushes, rugs, mats and doormats, a kind of rope and bottle brushes. From the tree itself are made helmets, caps and clog shoes. Furniture is made from the trunk and so are wood picture frames. From the roots come medicines, a beverage and dyes. Pickles are made out of the pith of the nut, called "ubod." So is a soup, "gunatan." A milky white drink, called "tuba," and vinegar come from the coco water. From the meat oil is pressed, and soap and glycerine, jam, lard, cocomilk, butter and "copra" are made. Copra, dried coconut, is one of the biggest industries of the islands. At first, as the meat dries in the sun, it smells like bread baking, and it is pleasant, but after a while you get so tired of it that you do not like it any more. From dried copra comes coconut oil.

The tuba drink which Filipinos enjoy very much is usually taken from the trees by boys. With their bolos, the knives which all country Filipinos carry in their belt and use for everything, boys cut steps in the trunk of the coconut tree. With a bamboo joint hung over their shoulders, they climb up and drain out the tuba juice into the bamboo joint. A favorite dance acts out the gathering of tuba sap.

Perhaps the straw for your new hat was raised in the Philippines. Besides straw and coconut, copra and rope and sugar, people buy many other things from the Philippines. Wrapping paper and tough Manila envelopes come from Filipino mills. Manila cigars—grown, dried and wrapped there—are sold all over the world. Baby dresses and caps, underwear and sheer handkerchiefs are embroidered by skilled girls very proud of their fine stitches. Around this page are pictures of some Filipino products being prepared for export.

Nimble-fingered girls weave handsome straw hats. As soon as a hat is woven, a man takes it and irons it smooth.

Wood pulp from enormous tropical forests is made into strong Manila paper and envelopes.

Girls in gay costumes gather leaves of fine tobacco to be made into Manila cigars.

BAMBOO

Bamboo, sugar, and salt

The feathery clusters of bamboo all through the jungles of the islands are nearly as important to Filipino life as the coconut. These hollow-stemmed jointed plants have been used since the earliest days to make knives and forks and eating bowls, as well as the walls and floors of nipa houses. Filipinos fish with bamboo poles, and their furniture is made from bamboo tied with rattan strips. Arches across the streets on fiesta days are made from the easily-bent bamboo. And the tiny new growing shoots are good to eat. A fire can be made without matches by a trick of rubbing two bamboo pieces together. Near Manila, toward the big Navy base at Cavite in a little village called Las Piñas, The Pines, there is a church organ made entirely of bamboo. It was made many years ago by a priest, and it can still be played today.

SALT

The sugar that you sprinkle on your cereal each morning probably came from either the Philippines or Puerto Rico. All over the Philippines there are huge fields of sugar cane, and big factories called sugar centrals, where the cane is pressed into syrup and cooked into the kind of sugar you use. The best sugar lands are in the Visayas. These are the islands of Panay, Negros, Cebu, Bohol, Leyte, and Samar.

There are large salt beds in many of the islands and many salt springs too. Filipinos often put small baskets and plates and other little things under these springs, so that they become coated with the drip from the salt springs and look like marble. In one of the provinces of Luzon, there is a mountain covered with salt so that it gleams in the sun for miles.

Trips into the country

Just as you, if you live in the city, like to take trips to the country, and if you live in the country, are always anxious to see the big cities, Filipino boys and girls look forward to traveling in their country. If you traveled in the islands, you would take your trips into the country by either automobile, or train, or boat. There are quite a few short railway lines in the islands, but their narrow-gauge rails are much closer together than the ones you are used to riding on.

As much as there is to do in Manila, there are some beautiful and exciting trips to take into the country in all parts of the islands. Some of these interesting trips are to the big volcanoes. Mount Mayon, the volcano on the twenty-peso note, is one of these. Mount Taal, almost on the doorstep of Manila, is another. Once this volcano had two lakes in its smoking crater, one bright red and the other bright green, but the last time Mount Taal erupted and ruined many towns nearby, the lakes disappeared. Old Taal

MOROS

is often called "the terrible" by the Filipinos. The highest volcano in the islands is Mount Apo on the southern island of Mindanao.

The Filipino Moro tribes live on part of the island of Mindanao. Moros also live on the islands called the Sulu Archipelago, where strange-looking birds called "boobies" flock on the beaches. Moros believe in the Mohammedan religion, and they have their own special kind of dress. They are famous for their swords, which they call a "kris." The Moros were living in the ancient city of Manila when the Spaniards first came to the Philippines. For many years they were a warlike people, but now they live peacefully with the other Filipinos and have their own representative in the Philippine Senate.

On the long island of Palawan, nearest the Asia coast, there is an exciting place to visit, even though it is hard to reach. That is the site of the famous river which runs underground for several miles.

A MORO WITH HIS KRIS

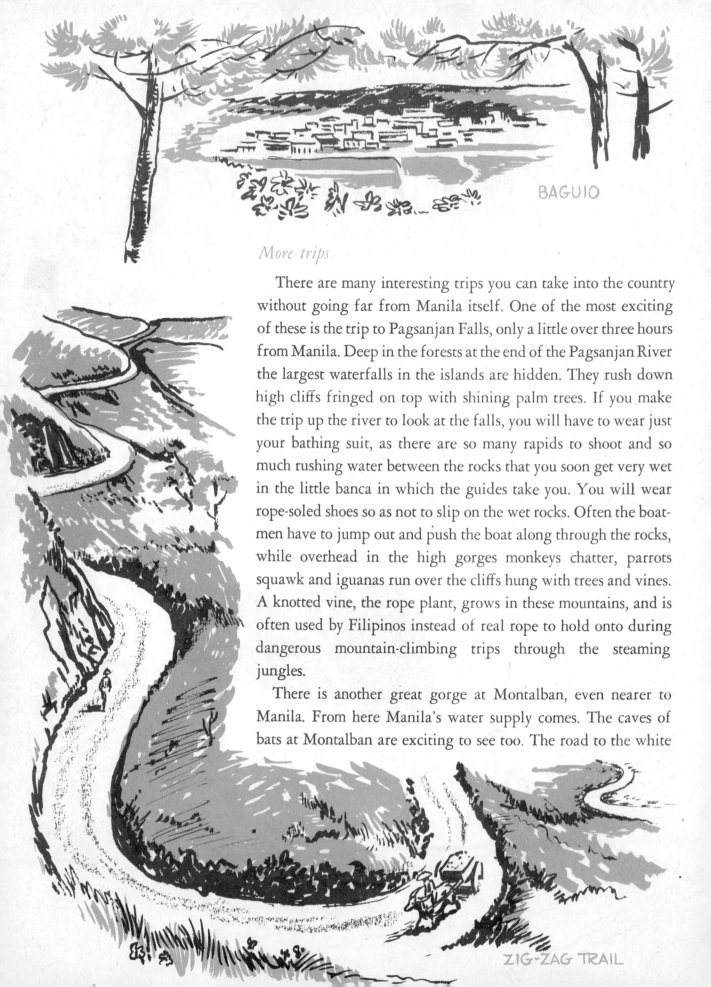

BAGUIO

More trips

There are many interesting trips you can take into the country without going far from Manila itself. One of the most exciting of these is the trip to Pagsanjan Falls, only a little over three hours from Manila. Deep in the forests at the end of the Pagsanjan River the largest waterfalls in the islands are hidden. They rush down high cliffs fringed on top with shining palm trees. If you make the trip up the river to look at the falls, you will have to wear just your bathing suit, as there are so many rapids to shoot and so much rushing water between the rocks that you soon get very wet in the little banca in which the guides take you. You will wear rope-soled shoes so as not to slip on the wet rocks. Often the boatmen have to jump out and push the boat along through the rocks, while overhead in the high gorges monkeys chatter, parrots squawk and iguanas run over the cliffs hung with trees and vines. A knotted vine, the rope plant, grows in these mountains, and is often used by Filipinos instead of real rope to hold onto during dangerous mountain-climbing trips through the steaming jungles.

There is another great gorge at Montalban, even nearer to Manila. From here Manila's water supply comes. The caves of bats at Montalban are exciting to see too. The road to the white

ZIG-ZAG TRAIL

limestone gorges rambles through the Mariquina Valley with its rolling green lands, pale green rice paddies and heavy dark shapes of mango trees beside the bright green of palms and bamboos.

Near this valley is the shrine of the Virgin of Antipolo, which thousands of Filipinos visit every year. This statue, dressed in a gold and jeweled dress, is very famous and is supposed to have calmed storms and come through fire. Once it was found in the top of an "antipolo" tree, the breadfruit tree, and that is how the statue got its name.

Perhaps the most beautiful trip of all is one high up in the mountains to the summer capital of Baguio, the Philippine name for typhoon. If you were an American boy and girl living in the Philippines, you might even go to school in Baguio all the year round because there is a special school for American boys and girls up on this Benguet mountain top. The road to Baguio winds higher and higher up into the cool pine mountains. The road has a sharp double curve that everyone calls "the Zig Zag." When you finally reach the top of the mountain, you come upon a beautiful white city planted with pines, roses, and white Benguet lilies. Baguio was planned by an architect from Chicago, and while many of its buildings were wrecked by the Japanese during the war, it is being rebuilt because it is the summer home of the Philippine government.

Fiestas, Philippine holidays

Holidays have always been important in the Philippines. They have most of the same holidays that you have, and there are some church holidays besides. June 19th is the birthday of their beloved José Rizal. December 30th is the day the Spaniards shot him on the field that is now the Luneta in Manila. December 30th is known as Heroes' Day. There is always a big parade on that day with beautiful floats, and a Filipina girl is elected queen.

Every town in the islands has a patron saint. On that saint's day in each town, there is a holiday with music and dancing and parades, and one of the girls from the town is chosen queen for the day. At fiesta-times, towns are filled with bamboo arches across the streets, covered with flowers. Everyone is out in the streets to celebrate, and there are street vendors selling food and candy, the big fluffs of bright-colored spun sugar on sticks, and "bocayo," the favorite candy of Filipino boys and girls. This is made by mixing brown sugar and coconut together.

The dancing always begins with the "rigodon," which the Spaniards brought to the islands from Spain long ago. It is very much like the Virginia reel. Judge Taft danced the rigodon at the first party he gave after he became governor of the Philippines. Everyone was surprised that he knew how to do it, but he had learned it before he ever left the United States because he knew it was a favorite dance of the Filipino people.

Christmas, the New Year, and Easter

Of all the holidays full of laughter and dancing and music, Easter is the quiet one. It is a religious day in the Philippines. There is never any Easter egg rolling or Easter bunnies to play with, for everyone thinks only about going to church that day. But everyone does wear new clothes, and Christmas day brings new clothes, too. There is the same long school vacation between Christmas and New Year that you have, and several days before Christmas the homes are decorated. But decorations are on the outside of the houses. In Manila, and in homes where Filipinos have gone to school in America and Europe, as many of them do, they may have Christmas trees with lights, and even eat turkey dinners. But out in the country, Christmas decorations are lanterns hung outside the house. Most of the lanterns are star-shaped.

During Christmas week boys and girls wander around in groups singing in front of the houses. They sing, not Christmas carols, but Philippine and Spanish songs, and many of the same ones you like to sing. They are given money at each house. After Christmas, the singers usually use the money to buy food for a picnic by the river, where they have a fine holiday afternoon of swimming.

On Christmas Day everyone goes to church early in the morning. When they come home from church, the boys and girls kiss the hands of their fathers and mothers. They also do this on

other days of the year—in the evening when the angelus bells ring out over the islands, and the family gathers together for its evening prayers before bedtime. This is an old Filipino custom.

Christmas dinner is a special one of barbecued pig stuffed with a particular stuffing of rice and spices. Rice and camotes are also served, and at the end there is a cake about two inches high, covered with coconut and brown sugar frosting. Then there are fruits and nuts. This is the favorite Easter dinner too. Relatives like to visit each other on these holidays and exchange presents. Usually these gifts are something to wear or to eat, money or books. Before schools close for the holidays, there are school Christmas parties where presents are exchanged, just as you do. These presents cost only a few centavos each, and are often dolls, candy, little balls, fans and small toys.

On New Year's Day, Filipino children like to make their own kind of firecracker to celebrate. They use a hollow bamboo pole for this. They stop up one end of it and tip the open end up a little. Then they make a hole in the side of the pole and pour in a little kerosene or oil. When they light the kerosene, it makes a big bang. Then they pour in more kerosene, light it, and there is another bang. They can use the same pole over and over.

IGORROTE DANCE

The Bahay Kubo dance

There is a dance in the Philippines that the smaller boys and girls like. They have a song that goes with it. The name of it is "Bahay Kubo," and it means My Nipa Hut. When they dance it, boys and girls are dressed like little farmers and carry baskets of vegetables. As they dance, they sing:

My nipa hut is very small

But in gathering seeds, see, it houses them all!

And when the planting time has come,

I can gather them all out of my little home.

Perhaps you would like to learn the chorus to the song just as the boys and girls your age sing it in the Philippine Tagalog language:

Sinkamas and talong, seguidillas and mani

Setaw, bataw, patani.

SALAKOT

BAHAY KUBO

Birthdays mean ice cream

First thing on the birthday morning, a Filipino boy or girl goes to church and next he is given the family presents. These are much the same as Christmas presents, just as yours are. Sometimes the present is a bicycle, if it has not been the Christmas present that year. The school class helps celebrate during the day, and after school the birthday boy or girl comes home to his favorite dinner, and usually ice cream for dessert. A big family party is held at dinner; relatives and friends come to help celebrate the day and bring presents.

A BAG FOR A MAN'S BIRTHDAY

The Carnival in Manila

February brings Carnival time in Manila. This is like the February Mardi Gras celebrations in New Orleans. All Manila is decorated with flowers, and people wear costumes and masks during the week. The Carnival grounds, near the Luneta, are full of big buildings for fun and gaiety, merry-go-rounds and ferris wheels and shooting galleries. All kinds of things grown and made in the Philippines are exhibited there by the different provinces, by the schools, and by business people. There are parades and dances in the evenings. And every moment of the day and night gay music sounds over the park. It is a very exciting time.

BUYING NEW CHINELLAS

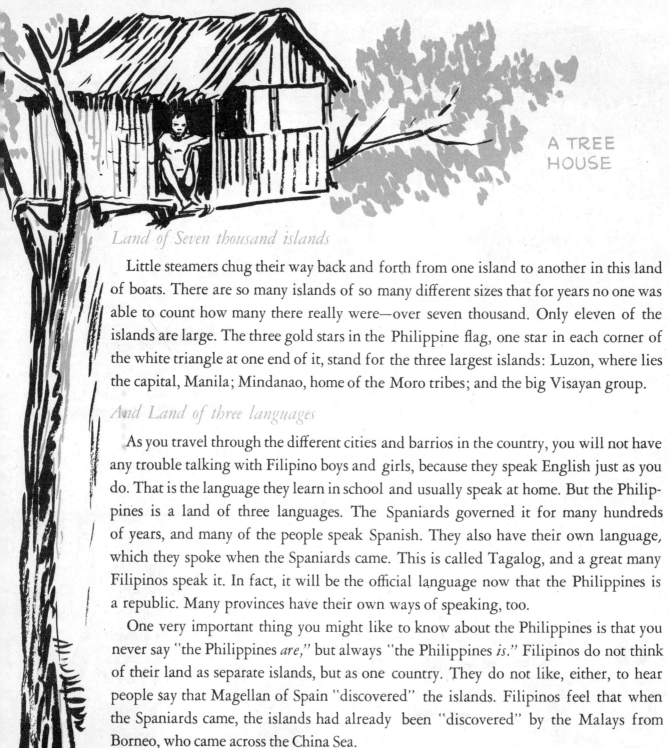

Land of Seven thousand islands

Little steamers chug their way back and forth from one island to another in this land of boats. There are so many islands of so many different sizes that for years no one was able to count how many there really were—over seven thousand. Only eleven of the islands are large. The three gold stars in the Philippine flag, one star in each corner of the white triangle at one end of it, stand for the three largest islands: Luzon, where lies the capital, Manila; Mindanao, home of the Moro tribes; and the big Visayan group.

And Land of three languages

As you travel through the different cities and barrios in the country, you will not have any trouble talking with Filipino boys and girls, because they speak English just as you do. That is the language they learn in school and usually speak at home. But the Philippines is a land of three languages. The Spaniards governed it for many hundreds of years, and many of the people speak Spanish. They also have their own language, which they spoke when the Spaniards came. This is called Tagalog, and a great many Filipinos speak it. In fact, it will be the official language now that the Philippines is a republic. Many provinces have their own ways of speaking, too.

One very important thing you might like to know about the Philippines is that you never say "the Philippines *are*," but always "the Philippines *is*." Filipinos do not think of their land as separate islands, but as one country. They do not like, either, to hear people say that Magellan of Spain "discovered" the islands. Filipinos feel that when the Spaniards came, the islands had already been "discovered" by the Malays from Borneo, who came across the China Sea.

A JUNK

The Filipino fight for freedom

Someone has been trying to conquer the Philippine Islands all through the hundreds of years that people have known about them. The first invaders were the Malays from Borneo. They came with their "dato" (chief) in swift boats they called "barangays." Up to that time a race of very small and very dark people had lived in the Philippines. When the Malays settled there, they brought many customs from the mainland of Asia with them, and they called their settlements barangays after their boats.

When the Spaniards came to the islands on their first surprise visit, they found many Chinese also settled there. Soon after the Spaniards came, the Japanese tried to conquer the islands, but they were driven back. A Chinese pirate by the name of Limahong raided Manila with thousands of troops. He was turned back, too. Then a Dutch fleet came, and there were some big battles. The largest was at Playa Honda, and the Hollanders nearly won that one and the Philippines with it. For a few months England held Manila during a war she was fighting with Spain.

But for most of the four hundred years until the Americans came, the Philippines was ruled by Spain. It was a harsh rule, and Filipinos in all of the islands rose up and fought against the Spaniards at every chance. Always they wanted to rule their country themselves, but it took them many hundreds of years to gain their freedom. Because of all the different nationalities in the islands, Filipinos usually have Spanish and often Chinese and American strains in them.

A GALLEON

From sailing boat to airplane

The Spaniards came to the Philippines in 1521. Admiral Magellan, who was in charge of five wooden Spanish ships, traveled across the Atlantic Ocean and around the tip of South America and then across the Pacific Ocean, all the way by sail. These were the first explorers to sail all the way around the world. It took Magellan's ships three months to cross the Pacific Ocean alone. The five ships were really looking for the Spice Islands. Instead, they found the Philippines. They conquered the islands in the name of the King of Spain. They named them for Prince Felipe of Spain, the Spanish name for Philip, and called them Las Felipenas.

Many years later, still under Spanish rule, the islands were allowed to trade only with Mexico, another important Spanish colony. Mexico also governed the Philippines. Big wooden flat-nosed ships with many silken sails were sent back and forth between Acapulco in Mexico and Manila in the Philippines. These huge ships were called galleons, and the two times each year they left Manila on the dangerous voyage to Mexico were great and joyous holidays. The bishops of Manila blessed the big ships and their precious cargoes of silken materials, fine carvings and precious stones from the Far East. Church bells rang, and the people sang and paraded through the streets. Big cannons boomed from the fortress on the shore. The galleon sails ballooned out

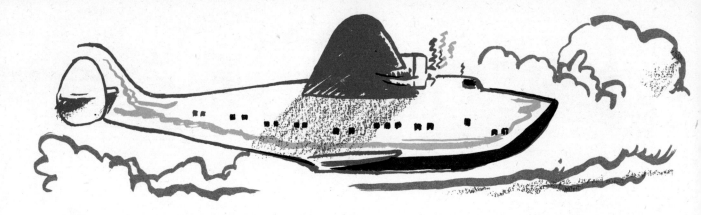

in the breezes of the monsoon winds, and off they sailed on their lonely long voyages to sell their cargo in Mexico.

On their homeward voyages to Manila they were loaded with heavy silver pesos from Mexico. It was those pesos that paid for the governing of the Philippines during the next year. Often galleons were lost at sea or pirates captured them. Then there was sorrow all over the islands, and the country was very poor until the next galleon came safely through the hard voyage. But when a galleon made the long trip to Mexico and back, there were wonderful celebrations in the islands. All Manila rushed to the harbor to welcome the great ship, church bells pealed all through the islands, there was singing and dancing, and at night people carrying lighted torches marched all through the city in big parades.

When the world began to use steamships and Spain allowed Manila to begin trading with other parts of the world, the galleons sailed no more. Steamships traveled across the Pacific in one month instead of the three months it had taken sailing ships. Many years later, in 1935, big clipper planes began to fly from San Francisco to Hongkong. They stopped at Manila on the way. In seven days they could fly from San Francisco in America to the far-off Philippines and China. The world was growing very small indeed. Now planes fly the big ocean even faster.

DEWEY'S FLEET

Filipino and American friendship

The Americans happened to come to the Philippines because in 1898 Spain and the United States were at war. An American Naval ship, the Maine, had been sunk in the harbor of Havana, Cuba, off the tip of Florida. Cuba belonged to Spain at this time. Commodore Dewey was ordered to sail down to the Spanish-ruled Philippines from Hongkong, where he had some American Naval ships, and to capture Manila for the United States. On a hot May morning, before the sun was up, he sailed into the wide blue harbor of Manila Bay with his five steel ships and two smaller ones. When daylight came, he could see from the bridge of his ship the Spanish fleet stretched out in front of Manila's white buildings with their red roofs. Five times Dewey ordered his ships to steam past the eight wooden Spanish boats, pelting fire at them from their big guns until the Spanish fleet sank. Dewey held Manila until American Army troops could be sent across the Pacific from San Francisco.

At first the Filipino people were very happy about the American victory. They had been fighting for many years for their freedom from Spain. They thought it had come at last and they could, after this, govern themselves. It was a great disappointment to them when they found that the United States planned to govern them. They began to fight against the American soldiers. Many of the young Filipino men and boys, who at first fought off the Americans so bitterly, later on became leaders in the new government which the United States set up in the islands. Forty years afterwards when the Japanese invaded the Philippines a second time, many of these same Filipinos fought willingly and with great bravery beside their American friends, to try to save their islands from the Japanese.

The Philippines for the Filipinos

When the Americans began to set up the new government for the Philippines back in 1900, the President of the United States, who was then William McKinley, chose Judge William Taft of Ohio to be the first governor. (A few years later Judge Taft was elected President of the United States). President McKinley told Judge Taft that he wanted him to govern the Philippines in the way that would be best for the Filipinos, and right at that time he promised the Philippines that just as soon as the Filipinos could govern themselves, the United States would set them free.

Judge Taft was a big kind jolly fat man. He liked the Filipino people and they loved him in return. After he had been there a little while, they called him Saint Taft. One of the first things Judge Taft did was to take over big plots of land which the Spaniards had taken away from the Filipinos long ago. He gave this land back to the Filipino people, who needed it for farms. Judge Taft and other Americans sent out to help him traveled over the islands and talked to the Filipino people to find out what they needed and how they felt about things. Nearly all of the people said they wanted most to be free and to govern themselves as the people of the United States did.

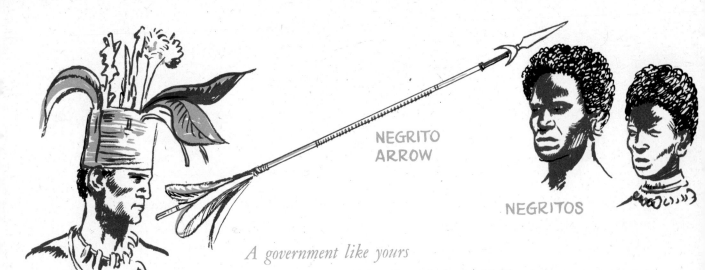

NEGRITO
ARROW

NEGRITOS

IFUGAO IN
CEREMONIAL
HEADDRESS

A government like yours

After the Spanish rule ended, the Philippine government was copied from the American government. Each province has its own governor, and each town its mayor. Since 1935, the Philippines has had its own president, who reported to the President of the United States each year, a resident commissioner who was in the United States congress in Washington, and an American governor. Later on, the governor was changed to the high commissioner of the Philippines. Men who served as high commissioner usually came back to the United States to be in the president's cabinet or on the supreme court, or to other high positions in the United States government in Washington. The Philippines had its own house of representatives and its own senate. Now, since Fourth of July, 1946, it is called the Republic of the Philippines instead of the Commonwealth of the Philippines, and the United States sends an ambassador instead of a high commissioner.

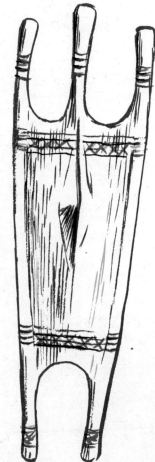

KALINGA SHIELD

IFUGAO GIRL

BAGOBO DRUM

MANGYAN

A BARONG

A MONTESE

Their own country

The color of the carnivals and fiestas is all part of the wonderful colors all over the Philippines, in everything its people do: in the gay pretty clothes they wear, in their bright painted boats and rainbow sails, in the green of the rice paddies and coconuts, and in the fruits and flowers of every color in the world.

These fine proud honorable people love color and beauty and music, but most of all they love their land. They love it so much that they never once stopped fighting for it in all the hundreds of years of invasion by other countries of the world. Their first invaders found the beautiful colors there, and even in those long-ago days they found a civilization far ahead of much of the rest of the world. The Filipino people's fight for freedom during these hundreds of years shows, in one small part of the world, everyone's fight to be free men and women and boys and girls. That is why there is such great joy in this beautiful island country that now, finally, after a long long struggle, the land is the Filipino's very own.

A MORO BRASS POT

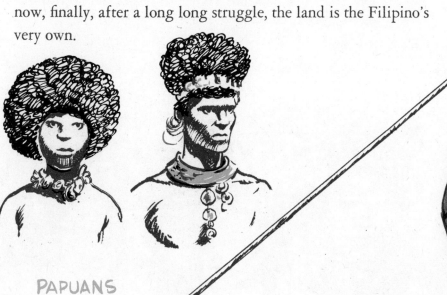

PAPUANS

IFUGAO SPEAR

TAGALOG POTTERY

TAGALOGS

PAPUAN

How to pronounce the words in this book

Acapulco	Ah kah *pool* koh	Limahong	Leem ah *hong*
Antipolo	Ahn tee *poh* loh	Luneta	Loo *nay* tah
Apo	*Ah* poh	Luzon	Loo *zohn*
Baguio	Bah ghee *oh*	Magellan	Mah *jel* lahn
Bahay Kubo	*Bah* hah ee *Koo* boh	Manuel Quezon	Mahn *well Kay* zohn
Bataan	Bah *tahn*	Manuel Roxas	Mahn *well Roh* hahs
Benguet	Ben *get*	Mariquina	Mah ree *kee* nah
Bohol	Boh *hole*	Mayon	Mah *yohn*
Calle	*Kahl* lyay	Mindanao	Min dah *nah* ow
Cebu	Say *boo*	Negros	*Nay* grohs
Colon	Koh *lohn*	Pagsanjan	Pahg san *hahn*
Corregidor	Koh *ray* hee dore	Palawan	Pah *lah* wahn
Felipe	Fay *lee* pay	Panay	Pah *nah* ee
Filipino	Fih lih *pee* noh	Pasig	*Pah* sig
Ideal	Ee day *ahl*	Playa Honda	*Plah* yah *On* dah
Ifugao	*Ee* foo *gah* ow	Samar	*Sah* mar
Iloilo	*Ee* loh *ee* loh	Santo Tomas	*Sahn* toh *Toh mahs*
Intramuros	Een trah *moo* rohs	Sulu	*Soo* loo
José Rizal	Hoh *zay* Ree *zahl*	Taal	Tah *ahl*
Laguna de Bay	Lah *goo* nah day *Bah* ee	Visayas	Vee *sah* yahs
Leyte	*Lay* tay	Zamboanga	Zam boh *ang* gah

TAGBANUA

MOROS

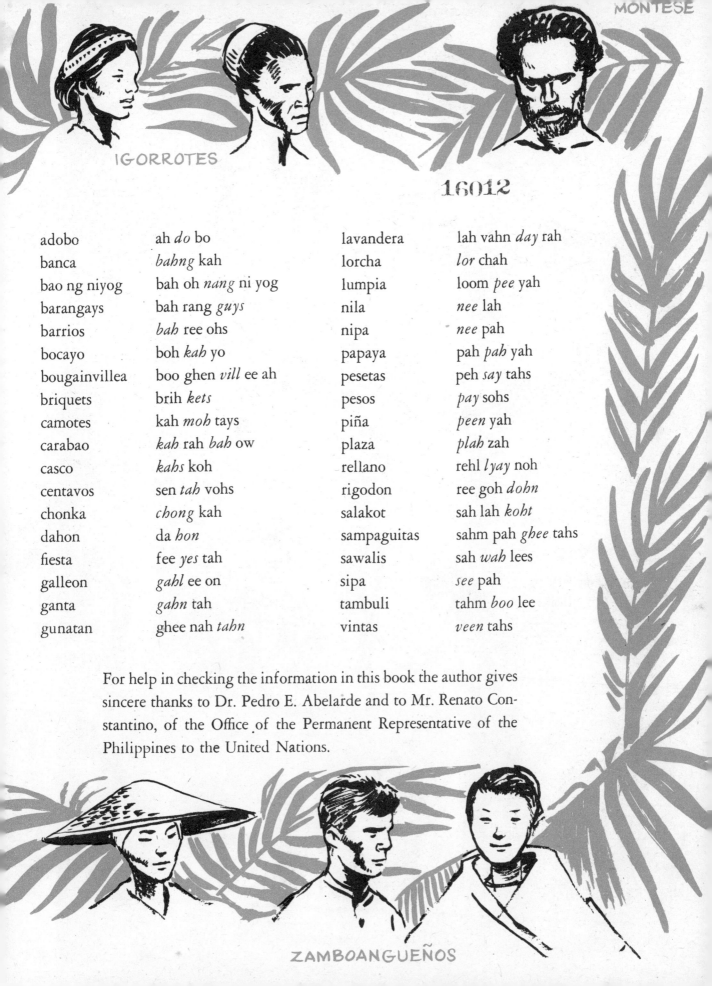

IGORROTES

MONTESE

16012

adobo	ah *do* bo	lavandera	lah vahn *day* rah
banca	*bahng* kah	lorcha	*lor* chah
bao ng niyog	bah oh *nang* ni yog	lumpia	loom *pee* yah
barangays	bah rang *guys*	nila	*nee* lah
barrios	*bah* ree ohs	nipa	*nee* pah
bocayo	boh *kah* yo	papaya	pah *pah* yah
bougainvillea	boo ghen *vill* ee ah	pesetas	peh *say* tahs
briquets	brih *kets*	pesos	*pay* sohs
camotes	kah *moh* tays	piña	*peen* yah
carabao	*kah* rah *bah* ow	plaza	*plah* zah
casco	*kahs* koh	rellano	rehl *lyay* noh
centavos	sen *tah* vohs	rigodon	ree goh *dohn*
chonka	*chong* kah	salakot	sah lah *koht*
dahon	da *hon*	sampaguitas	sahm pah *ghee* tahs
fiesta	fee *yes* tah	sawalis	sah *wah* lees
galleon	*gahl* ee on	sipa	*see* pah
ganta	*gahn* tah	tambuli	tahm *boo* lee
gunatan	ghee nah *tahn*	vintas	*veen* tahs

For help in checking the information in this book the author gives sincere thanks to Dr. Pedro E. Abelarde and to Mr. Renato Constantino, of the Office of the Permanent Representative of the Philippines to the United Nations.

ZAMBOANGUEÑOS